THE MARQUIS DE SADE

Borgo Press Books by FRANK J. MORLOCK

The Marquis de Sade: A Play in Two Acts, by Charles Méré

THE MARQUIS DE SADE

A PLAY IN TWO ACTS

CHARLES MÉRÉ

Translated and Adapted by Frank J. Morlock

THE BORGO PRESS

MMXI

THE MARQUIS DE SADE

FIRST EDITION

Published by Wildside Press LLC

www.wildsidebooks.com

DEDICATION

To the Divine Marquis himself,

As none else is as deserving or
at least willing to admit being so.

CONTENTS

CAST OF CHARACTERS

Monsieur de Sade
Royer-Collard, head doctor at Charenton
Dubourg, de Sade's lackey
Regnier, Police Inspector
Brissac, Police Inspector
The Director of Charenton Hospital
The Jacobin
The Priest
Micoulet
A Hospital Guard
La Pierre, de Sade's lackey
Perrault, Police Inspector (mute character)
Caron, Police Inspector (mute character)
La Fanchon
Delphine
La Saint Ange
La Dubois
Madame de Rochebrune
Marie
Justine

The first act takes place in Paris in de Sade's home in 1801.

The second act in the hospice of Charenton in 1808.

ACT I

De Sade's home. A room richly decorated with multiple mirrors. Table in the middle, luxuriously appointed; crystal, silver ware and flowers. To the right, near the audience, a window. In the rear a loggia. In the loggia, a sofa. Above the sofa a picture representing a faun paused before a sleeping, naked woman. Two double doors, one at the back, the other at the left, in cutaway, opening on a salon. Between the loggia and the door at the right, a screen. Chimney to the left. Torches and chandeliers lit up.

De Sade, La Saint Ange, and Delphine are dining. It's the end of supper. In Roman costumes, the women are half naked, they are laughing nervously. La Saint Ange is opulent, of expansive beauty; Delphine is younger, a superb reddish-blonde girl.

DE SADE

(raising his glass)

And thanks to you, Saint Ange, beauty of beauties! You, the priestess of saturnalias at Barras's! You, powerful! Honored! Respected! (she titters) Control yourself, you're drunk! (he continues) You, the New Juliette! Or "The Prosperity of Vice"— Ah! It's indeed you! Thanks for having come, so that my sweet friend Delphine, my student entreated you. (laughter) Love on the double has always been repugnant to me for its grossness! (they laugh) It's short and beastly, the equal of what animals do! Unworthy of sensitive hearts! I drink to intelligent, divine love!

LA SAINT ANGE

I adore you, Marquis!

DE SADE

Shush! Not "Marquis." The First Consul doesn't like aristocrats!

LA SAINT ANGE

(laughing)

Would you prefer, so as to heat up your head, for me to call you rogue or swindler?

DE SADE

(rising)

Call me Sade! (he drinks) On the subject of Bonaparte!—do you know he still has it in for me? (La

Saint Ange says "Yes") What stupidity! (he points to a book on the chimney) For that! That innocent novel: Zoloe and her two acolytes! (with pride) A free writer like me, played at the Théâtre-Français!

DELPHINE

Yes—but Josephine was recognized in Zoloe!

LA SAINT ANGE

And Tallien in Laureda!

DELPHINE

And Barras in the Vicomte!

LA SAINT ANGE

And Bonaparte in Orsec!

DELPHINE

And you show them abandoning themselves in a little house.

DE SADE

(laughing)

Bah! Like here!

LA SAINT ANGE

—To foul libertinage! Bonaparte! Oh! (she laughs)

DE SADE:

You please me! And what can Bonaparte do to me? Throw me in prison? I lived there fourteen years. Fourteen years of forced chastity, in which the worst instincts in me became infuriated! Fourteen years in a cell in which I was capable of becoming—mad! (shaking his fist) Executioners! The Castle of Saumer! Mirolans! The dungeon of Vincennes and The Bastille! Thanks, Capet! At last the dawn of the Republic came. Me, the friend of the great Marat, member of the section of Spades—they found me very moderate! (laughter from the women) In prison! At Madelonnettes! And then at Carmes! And Picpus! (he laughs) Where would Bonaparte incarcerate me? Ah! What sweet liberty in this philosophic century!

LA SAINT ANGE

(gaily)

Scapegrace! You are forgetting your crimes!

DE SADE:

(eyes to heaven)

My crimes! (he leans toward her and embraces her)

Give me your mouth! (he embraces Delphine) And you, yours!

(in a gallant tone he declaims)

One is not a criminal for making a painting

Of the bizarre inclinations that Nature inspires!

LA SAINT ANGE

But you lived them, swine, your novels! You only love the fair sex in a bloody condition (De Sade laughs and says "Eh!") You martyrize women!

DE SADE

Exaggeration!

DELPHINE

Defiled—poisoned!

DE SADE

My enemies said so!

LA SAINT ANGE

But you did it!

DE SADE

Others have done it! I knew Charolais, Fronsac, de Richelieu, in the fine days of the Stag Park! I read Monsieur de Mirabeau! I saw Barras!

LA SAINT ANGE

(gaily)

Less of a rogue than you, the professor of vice!

DELPHINE

(she is seated, leaning on the table, and with a sort of horror)

Ah! The Demon!

DE SADE

Because I am a philosopher, that's why! I am continuing Hobach de la Mettrie! It's not enough to experience sensations. Sometimes it's nicer to know how to talk about them than to enjoy them. And when one can no longer do this, it is divine to cast responsibility on another!

DELPHINE

(as if to herself)

And they love him. They know he's criminal, perverse— They weep over him, over his misfortune—Sometimes they detest him too! And despite himself they love him. (she starts to weep)

DE SADE

(laughs)

Why, she's weeping! My word! (laughs) She's had too much to drink! (he wants to caress her, she escapes) And there's my tender Delphine! My latest conquest, Saint Ange! I knew her when she was a child. I really loved her mother! an admirable woman! Show your eyes! Delphine! She was boring and sulky Virtue; I made of her a Vestal of Vice! (he kisses her)

DELPHINE

Ah, Shut up! (she disengages herself)

DE SADE

(he's rejoined her)

She's weeping, thinking of paradise lost!

LA SAINT ANGE

(hovering over Delphine)

Oh! And the heat, the wine! Leaver her alone!

DE SADE

(he takes Delphine's wrists; she recoils)

Virtue captured by Vice! What a beautiful subject for painters of allegory! Adorable Delphine! An angelic soul in a she-devil's heart! Her soul's revolted and hates me! But the she-devil loves me: she's my daughter!

(he bursts into laughter and holding them both by the wrists, pulls them to him)

Let's love at the moment of awakening!

Let's love at the rise of the dawn!

Let's love when the Sun goes down!

During the night, let's love yet again!

(The women disengage, screaming "No! No!" But de Sade bangs his fist on the table and changes his tone.)

DE SADE

Well! And the surprise?

LA SAINT ANGE

Ah, yes! Indeed! The surprise!

DELPHINE

(drying her eyes)

What is it?

DE SADE

(he looks at them, then points to the door at the right)

It's there!

LA SAINT ANGE

(looking at the door)

There?

DE SADE

Behind the door!

DELPHINE

But who?

LA SAINT ANGE

What?

DE SADE

The surprise of this supper? (snickering) Ah! Ah! Your

eyes are shining Saint Ange (to Delphine) And you are not weeping any more, you slut! The surprise? It's a mysterious unknown joy or misfortune, no one knows! But your heart's beating, your head's lit up! You've got fever—you want to know, right? Or see?

DELPHINE

(looking at Saint Ange)

What has he conceived this time?

DE SADE

The supper was brilliant, correct? A clever debauch! I love audacious gestures! (he calls, in a voice suddenly changed, somber, brutal) Dubourg!

(The door at the left opens. Dubourg and Lapierre enter. Two lackeys, two giants, with low brows, bestial faces. Instinctively La Saint Ange and Delphine make gestures of terror. De Sade looks at them with an ironic smile.)

DE SADE

(stopping the two women in their hurried curtsies of flight)

Well, what?

(He makes a sign to Lapierre to clear the table. Lapierre

obeys with the gestures of an automaton. A silence. There's nothing left on the table but a white napkin. De Sade looks alternatively from the lackeys to the women a grin at the corner of his lips)

LA SAINT ANGE

(troubled)

Finally? What's the (she doesn't finish—pointing to the door at the right) A diversion?

DE SADE:

(cutting her off)

I'm trying to find the word!

LA SAINT ANGE

(uneasily)

A diversion—gallant? Or prudish?

DE SADE

(enigmatic)

Both.

DELPHINE

(uneasily)

Ah! Nothing wild, especially?

(De Sade makes a negative gesture of the head.)

LA SAINT ANGE

Word of honor?

DE SADE

(with the accent of a fop)

My little word of honor!

(Lapierre has gone out. Dubourg remains on stage, holding himself motionless before the table. De Sade looks at him)

Well, Dubourg?

(he approaches him, scrutinizes him with a silent grin)

Good dog, Dubourg (he points to the door at the right) Still there?

DUBOURG

(with motionless rigidity)

Still.

DE SADE

(after a little laugh)

And she hasn't asked anything? Said anything?

DUBOURG

Nothing.

DE SADE

In the same place where I made her sit?

DUBOURG

In the same place.

DE SADE

(with a cruel smile)

And—she hasn't died of cold in that icy corridor?

DUBOURG

She's waiting.

DE SADE

(Sending him away with an abrupt gesture)

Go!

(Dubourg leaves by the left.)

LA SAINT ANGE

After all who is this?

DELPHINE

Who?

DE SADE

A woman was lacking at this party! There are only two of you! Now I adore odd numbers! I've invited (he stops)

DELPHINE AND SAINT ANGE

(together)

Why, speak! Who?

DE SADE

(sitting smiling at the corner of the table to the left)

Before coming to this supper I went to a Public Ball! What balls Paris has this year! The women that go there are half naked in their Roman costumes—

LA SAINT ANGE

Your dream!

DE SADE

The way they dance, in Paris, the way they dance! They dance for eighty sous per cavalier, a dozen sous for Female Citizens, rue Filles-Saint-Thomas! They dance all the Fifth Days and Tenth days at rue Thionville! They dance the dance of Paphos at rue Temple! At Calypso's in Montmartre They dance at the Hotel China! They dance everywhere! (impatiently, the two women want to interrupt him two or three times, he continues, determined to make them wait.) Life is horribly expensive! A pair of slippers is worth 200 pounds!

DELPHINE AND SAINT ANGE

But—

DE SADE

But they dance! They don't know if they'll be living tomorrow! And, as for me, I've seen red tomorrows! They dance, while waiting to die!

LA SAINT ANGE

(talking as the same time as Delphine)

But (pointing to the door at the right) you told us—!

DELPHINE

In the end, who is this woman?

DE SADE

So curious! I'm getting there! I noticed, at the Ball, at Calypso's, one of the girls who was dancing! Oh! Lifelessly! I followed her outside, questioned her. The wretched woman! Under her scanty clothes, she was shivering because of this winter night. She hadn't eaten since morning. I treated her with softness, with tenderness— I proposed to bring her here to my place where she would find a good supper good shelter! I gave her a little money. She accepted. She's there. Make room for her ladies! She's a prostitute!

DELPHINE AND LA SAINT ANGE

(shocked and indignant)

Oh!

DELPHINE

That woman.

LA SAINT ANGE

With us!

DE SADE

Well—There'll be three of you (going to the door at the left and calling) Dubourg!

LA SAINT ANGE

That girl, here, it's shameful!

DELPHINE

Yes, indeed! Shameful!

LA SAINT ANGE

(repeating forcefully)

Shameful.

DE SADE

(has spoken a few words to Dubourg in a low voice, in the half open doorway, then he returns to the two women and dominates them with his voice)

Ah, indeed! The beauties! What's that you are saying? Despite your reputation, despite your luxury, despite your gold! Let's find the word!— Hookers! (they are indignant) What? You Saint Ange, you sold yourself to Barras, to Fessinot! You have rich lovers! The price doesn't change the nature of the thing!

LA SAINT ANGE

(indignant)

Cynic!

DE SADE

(continuing)

Anyway—hookers? Creatures of love that public opinion withers, but that sensuality crowns! (half mocking, half lyrical) The National Assembly freed you! We are returning to the ancient traditions of Aphrodite! Honor to the fille de joie, goddess of reason!

LA SAINT ANGE

Call her goddess if you like: what do you intend to do?

DELPHINE

Indeed, yes—what do you intend to do?

DE SADE

You are going to see!

(the door at the right opens. Dubourg is to be seen pushing Fanchon on stage and locking the door)

(Fanchon is twenty years old. She's a beautiful girl

with a simple heart. She enters recoiling, looking with terror at Dubourg. The door is shut behind her. Fanchon turns, notices de Sade and the two women. She experiences a moment of shame.)

FANCHON

(timidly)

Oh! Pardon—

DE SADE

Why? Pardon? Come closer! Don't be afraid. The ladies are my friends! They only wish you well! How do you like my place?

FANCHON

(looking about)

Oh! It's beautiful (a pause) The temperature is nice.

DE SADE

Warmer than at the Ball at Calypso's huh?

FANCHON

(with a smile)

Oh, yes! Monsieur!

DE SADE

What's your name?

FANCHON

Fanchon, sir!

DE SADE

(he touches her chin and winks knowingly at her, then to his friends)

What a beautiful girl, huh? (he examines her) I really like this savage costume and her hairstyle *à la* Caracalla?

(abruptly) Show your breasts!

(Fanchon, surprised pulls her kerchief to her neck)

She has admirable eyes! And that red mouth—like a wound!

(the expression on De Sade's face becomes hard, passionate)

And those shoulders—so white—so white (he walks around her) Without stigmata—without a birthmark.

(these words in a heavy, bitter voice, make Fanchon draw back)

FANCHON

Oh! Why, sir, I—

DE SADE

(looking at Fanchon's shoulders with strange eyes)

Yes!

(She recoils a step, terrified. He smiles and with sweetness)

Sit down!

(A pause. She sits.) I asked you to show us your breasts!

(Fanchon looks at him uneasily) Modesty?

(to Saint Ange and Delphine) How tenacious prejudice is, isn't it? Even in a prostitute Oh! Because you are!

(roughly and suddenly he tears off Fanchon's kerchief)

You're ashamed?

(Fanchon gets loose)

What a stupid girl!

(Frightened gestures by Delphine and Saint Ange)

FANCHON

(having risen)

I ask your pardon, sir! You were so good, so nice when you spoke to me there—I thought that you simply had pity on me and that—in the end, that—it was not a question of— (Gesture by de Sade) Oh! I know perfectly well (She tosses her head) Pity is so rare in men! (tears come to her eyes)

DELPHINE

(low)

The poor thing!

DE SADE

(in a harsh tone that ends in a crescendo)

So you sell yourself? You sell your skin to men? For what price?

FANCHON

(lowering her head)

Only for the last two months, sir, have I fallen so low! My lover abandoned me. He's in the army of the Rhine. No news—no money! I didn't find any work. I was hungry, and—(she concludes with a desperate gesture)

DE SADE

(harshly, he seizes her arm)

And you are prostituting yourself? Your mouth, your body to whoever pays for them! The passer-by, be he young or old, repugnant or handsome, you make a sign, right? And you offer yourself! What shame—

FANCHON

(collapsing in tears)

Ah! Sir!

DE SADE

Do you pay for your sin? You have no remorse! Don't you fear hell? Or the strict justice of virtuous men? (with savage threat) You deserve to be beaten! And to be punished! For you sullied love! And dishonored kissing!

DELPHINE

(low to de Sade)

Leave her alone! What an atrocious comedy!

DE SADE

(fist raised, to Fanchon)

Wretch! You come from mud!

FANCHON

Sir!

DE SADE

(ferocious)

From mud!

FANCHON

(getting away)

Ah, sir! Sir! Let me go away! I am choking from pain and shame! Why—why did you make me come? Punished? Ah! I am, go! In my life, in my flesh! I've expiated my sin in disgust. I thought I read in your eyes, kindness, sweetness. I thought—I was stupid!— that you were going to come to my aid, find me work, a place to live—did I know! And you are condemning me, that's fair! (with a scream) Still sir, still—if you knew! Ah, for me joy is dead—and hope, dead—and love, dead! (in despair) Love that the rest of you talk about!—I ask your pardon—I'm going away, I'm going away— I'm returning to my mud as you say—to— my—mud—to—to—(she can no longer speak; tears choke her. She weeps) Ah! This is horrible!

DE SADE

(as she speaks, his eyes shining with an evil joy. To Delphine and to Saint Ange, with a strange laugh, pointing to Fanchon who is weeping)

Well! Well? The surprise? (laughing) Ah! Ah! Ah! (to Fanchon) Come on! Come on! Don't cry any more! (with an expression of unspeakable cruelty) I forgive you—! (pause) Don't cry any more! We won't speak about that any more—isn't that so, miladies? It's over! (Fanchon makes a gesture of going to the door at the left. He stops her) I frighten you? (unctuously) You don't trust me?

FANCHON

(fear growing in her)

I don't know, sir.

DE SADE

(eyes shining)

I am good! Honest! (calling in a brutal voice) Dubourg!

(The two lackeys enter from the left)

DE SADE

(to Fanchon)

Are you hungry? Are you thirsty! Order what you want!

FANCHON

(fear under her smile)

Thanks, sir, thanks—I prefer to go away (again she wants to flee)

DE SADE

(holding her by the arm, brutally)

No!

(Fanchon shakes)

Why you are trembling. (with a sinister smile) Dubourg! A glass of spirits for madame!

(Dubourg obeys. Fanchon takes the glass from Dubourg's hands, trembling)

You can drink (he smiles) It's not poison.

(Fanchon doesn't drink, she's afraid)

You're afraid. Look!

(Dubourg pours a glass for himself, and drinks. Fanchon, in her turn, drinks)

That warms you up, right? (a pause) Then you are no longer afraid?

FANCHON

(taking courage, but hesitating)

No, sir!

DE SADE

Then smile! Smile, will you!

(Fanchon smiles a forced smile, uneasily) There!

(To Delphine and Saint Ange) Well there at last— she's smiling! (he recoils, takes the field, like a painter before his picture, he laughs and looks at Fanchon, but suddenly his face becomes terrible, and with a brutal gesture to Dubourg and Lapierre he howls) Grab her!

(Dubourg and Lapierre rush Fanchon, master her. Fanchon shocked, screams. Delphine and Saint Ange scream, too, in terror.)

FANCHON

(struggling)

Ah! Help me! Let me go!

DE SADE

(to the lackeys)

There! On the table!

(The lackeys stretch Fanchon on the table, one holding her feet, the other her wrists.)

DELPHINE

Why, you are mad!

LA SAINT ANGE

De Sade!

DE SADE

(going towards them)

Silence! You!

FANCHON

(held down, clamoring)

Help! Help me! Help!

DE SADE

The gag!

(Dubourg gags her with a napkin. She struggles, choking and screaming. De Sade leans over her.)

And don't scream! Don't budge! Or you are dead!

DELPHINE

Why, this is monstrous! Leave her alone!

LA SAINT ANGE

Let her go!

DE SADE

Peace, the rest of you! (threateningly) If not, Dubourg! And it's your turn, Delphine! And you, yours, Saint Ange! I am the master!

(He circles the table looking at Fanchon) Look at her! Ah! What silence now.

FANCHON

(through her gag)

Pity! Pity! Pity!

DE SADE

(leaning over her)

Hush! (she shuts up. he looks at her) You'd say absolutely, a savage beast taken in a trap. Are you a hunter, Dubourg? Look! Who will deny this identity of man and animal? (exalting) You've never seen a wounded hind, miladies? See—the animality of this throat, these fixed haggard eyes—in which you can only read fear, bestial fear! We might have taken a panther in some hunting trap. (laughing) That's it completely. We've got the female, Dubourg! The beast shivers to baying hounds. Talley ho! Talley ho! Talley ho!

DELPHINE

(shocked)

Untie her! Enough.

DE SADE

(to Delphine, brutally)

If I was cruel, as much as they said, this living animal—is mine!

(to Fanchon, as he leans over her) You would be hanged! Broken on the wheel! Drawn and quartered! Burned alive!

FANCHON

(struggling, shocked)

Ah! Ah! Ah! Ah!

DE SADE

The torches, Dubourg! The torches!

(with a brutal gesture he tears off Fanchon's dress. Her nudity appears. Dubourg has placed the torch on the table behind Fanchon's shoulder)

FANCHON

(with a start at the sight of the flame)

Ah! Ah!

DE SADE

You're not cold? (with a sign to Dubourg) Dubourg! (to Fanchon) Don't be afraid! It's not an executioner who's speaking to you but a philosopher! (gravely) Take seats, miladies! Take seats!

(Dubourg has brought a box, He opens it. He takes out a scalpel, and hand raised holds the instrument between the skin and the index finger. Pointing towards Fanchon)

What's this wretched woman doing on the earth? She must serve us to decipher all the mysteries of the human structure— (scalpel in hand he comes and goes, talking all the while before the stunned women) What is the soul? Matter! The movement and the collision of molecules explain everything! The soul conforms to the impressions of the body! It is feeble in adolescence, weaker in old age! It succumbs to all the perils that menace the body— Thus matter! Matter! Matter!— and if I bring the scalpel closer—

FANCHON

(looking at the steel with stunned aversion)

Ah! Ah!

DELPHINE AND LA SAINT ANGE

Ah!

DE SADE

(ferociously to Fanchon)

So, you've never seen a surgeon! Look! Delphine! Saint Ange!

DELPHINE

(averting her eyes with terror)

Ah! This is atrocious! Ah!

DE SADE

(placing the scalpel by Fanchon's heart)

If I shove it in—the scalpel.

FANCHON

(with a great scream)

Ah! (she gets loose with a superhuman effort, sitting up) Ah! Pity! Not that! Not that!

DE SADE

Hold her tight, Dubourg! (the lackeys hold her) Have no fear, Fanchon! You are beautiful! Zounds! I have to kiss you! (he brings his lips close to Fanchon, she weakens and faints) She fainted—fainted before I touched her! The soul's asleep, but I can wake her up! (he brings the scalpel to her shoulder)

DELPHINE AND LA SAINT ANGE

Ah! Enough! Enough! Pity!

DE SADE

(sneering)

And the animal, miladies? Are you thinking of it? The defenseless animal, submissive to the caprice of anatomic dissection! Of vivisection? Like this? (he slices her)

FANCHON

Ha!

DE SADE

(he slices her)

Like this!

FANCHON

(howling with misery)

Ha! Ha! Ha!

DUBOURG

She's going to wake the Watch!

DE SADE

Slut!

FANCHON

(who's succeeded in getting the gag loose)

Help! Help! Help me!

DE SADE

(furious)

Take her into the laboratory!

(Dubourg and Lapierre take her away to the left.)

(De Sade wants to follow them Delphine and La Saint Ange bar his way, stopping him)

DELPHINE

Ah! That's enough of that! Ah! Leave her alone!

LA SAINT ANGE

Delphine's right! It's a crime!

DE SADE

(unhinged)

Is it a crime to obey one's nature? Nature, egoistic and barbaric, God!

DELPHINE

Cruel!

(they stride toward him, forcing him to recoil)

DE SADE

But we are born cruel, with the instinct of destruction, the love of evil! The child breaks his toy! Gnaws the breast of its mother! Strangles birds!

DELPHINE

Horror!

DE SADE

(striding towards them in his turn, forcing them to recoil)

Shut up! You are more cruel than we! Let them announce an atrocious spectacle, a battle, an execution, women rush to it en masse! Their screams, their excitement? Hypocrites! Sensuality that they taste, they deny, until the final admission—when they swoon!

DELPHINE

In the end, what do you intend? To kill her?

(Fanchon is heard howling, off)

DE SADE:

She's calling me, you hear?

(He tries to pass, they prevent him)

DELPHINE AND LA SAINT ANGE

No! No! No!

(De Sade raises the scalpel he holds in his hand against them)

DELPHINE

Ah!

DE SADE

(scalpel raised)

Too late! I intend for them to see! And remain! I wish it!

(He forces them to leave by the left. A pause. One can hear Fanchon screaming. The stage is deserted. But suddenly, at the window on the right, the noise of a shutter opening outside. The glass shatters. A hand passes through the opening, and opens the window, A man climbs through, pistol in hand.)

REGNIER

(to Brissac)

Go! Follow me, you! (by the window in the corridor) Perrault and Caron, to the exits of the garden! And shoot anyone escaping.

(Brissac has entered, following Regnier)

Ah! This time—

(he's stopped by a scream from Fanchon off)

FANCHON

Ah! Ah!

REGNIER

(to Brissac)

Listen (he cups his ear) Somebody!

(They hide behind the screen, de Sade enters, haggard, staggering as if drunk. He looks at his hands covered with blood.)

DE SADE

(to himself in growing exaltation)

Smell of blood! Which intoxicates the wild beast! The pack that's hunting! The crowd that kills! (with a shriveled laugh) Screams of torture, or screams of love, it's the same thing!

FANCHON

(off)

Ah…ah!

DE SADE

(sneering)

Ah! Ah! Scream, my lover! Scream your pain! Suffering and joy speak the same language! Ice or fire, good and evil, burn alike. (distracted) Now I must put this down—write—yes, that's it to confound the theists, the philanthropists! (he goes to a writing box placed on the chimney) To confound them with—the scalpel! (Suddenly he stops, recoiling, as he notices Regnier in the mirror with his pistol trained on him, advancing. He turns) Who are you?

REGNIER

Inspector of police!

(gesture by de Sade) Don't resist, I'll shoot!

(the two inspectors aim at him.)

DE SADE

(haughtily)

Do you know who I am?

REGNIER

Yes! De Sade! You're under arrest! (taking a paper from his pocket) I have the warrant! (still holding de Sade in respect, to Brissac) Go! Search the house! You!

(Brissac hurries out to the left. Loud voices off are heard during what follows. The light at the left flickers out.)

DE SADE

You're arresting me? By what right! On whose order?

REGNIER

Ask the First Consul! (he reads the warrant) The Prefect of Police authorizes and orders the concierge of the Maison de Saint Pélagie to receive and to detain until a new order, the named De Sade.

DE SADE

(with fury)

And why? Why? A Bonaparte's response to Zoloe? Prisoner of state? A *lettre de cachet*, without a valid judgment and without any reason given?

REGNIER

We're looking for a reason!— There is one!

(At this moment, the voice of Brissac off to the left)

BRISSAC

Go! Go! Off with you! (he pushes Delphine and Saint Ange on stage in front of him. To Regnier) The men jumped out the window. There were two of them!

REGNIER

We'll catch them! (a shot off.) There!

(The two men and women have retreated, shocked, to the window at the right. At the sound of the gunshot they scream in terror. At this moment two other police appear at the door to the right, Perrault and Caron.)

DELPHINE

(to Regnier)

Ah! Sir! Sir! There's a woman here who must be rescued right away!

LA SAINT ANGE

(supplicating)

Oh, yes! Save her! Quick!

BRISSAC

What woman?

REGNIER

The one who screamed, for god's sake!

BRISSAC

They put out the light when I entered. I didn't see anything!

DELPHINE

(shattered)

Yes! Yes! There! In the room at the back! She's stretched on a board—to the right. She's not screaming any more! She's not screaming any more!

REGNIER

(to Brissac)

Go! Take the torch! Go!

(Brissac leaves by the left, torch in hand.)

DELPHINE

(pale, voiceless, trembling, pressing against La Saint

Ange)

Ah! listen! She's not screaming any more! She is dead!

LA SAINT ANGE

(in shock)

Dead?

(A silence. De Sade remains motionless as if in a dream)

REGNIER

(he moves the table to clear the stage, and in a loud voice to Brissac who is still off)

Well?

BRISSAC

A naked woman.

REGNIER

(to Brissac)

Dead—or living?

BRISSAC

(leaning over Fanchon, feeling her heart)

Alive!

REGNIER

Well, help her! (he leans over Fanchon) Go! Look! Woman!— You are wounded! Come on! Try! Come to! Get up!

(Regnier and Brissac stand Fanchon up. At the sight of men she has a reaction of shock. She is distracted by the gesture Regnier makes toward her.)

FANCHON

Ah!

BRISSAC

Don't be afraid of us, Police! You are saved! (Fanchon has retreated to the table, eyes haggard) Who are you?

REGNIER

What's your name?

(She makes no response)

BRISSAC

Well, what!? Speak! Say your name! You're mute?

FANCHON

(looking at them stupidly, then noticing her arms and shoulders covered in blood, she screams)

Blood! Blood! Ah! Ah! Ah!

(She howls and her howling changes to laughter in a frenetic laugh.)

REGNIER

Ah, so that's it! She's mad!

BRISSAC

Tie 'em up!

REGNIER

(to his men)

Go! Perrault! Carron! You take the mad woman!

(to Brissac, pointing to de Sade)

And the two of us will take them all along.

(The inspectors throw themselves on Fanchon, who laughs, howls, and struggles, as the curtain falls)

CURTAIN

ACT II

DE SADE's room in the Charenton hospital.

A cell locked by a large barred gate at the back opening on a corridor. Door to the left and right giving on a corridor. On stage, at the right a camp light, to the left a small table and stool. On the table, a writing box, books. The stage is dimly lit. The light comes from the corridor on whose doorway is hung a lantern. The lantern is lit. It is five o'clock in the evening.

AT RISE, the stage is deserted. In the corridor a woman can be heard screaming, then more screams, deafening stamping of feet, the habitual bacchanal of mad houses. Five o'clock strikes on a distant clock. The Director enters from the back followed by Royer-Collard.

DIRECTOR

(seeing the empty cell)

Five o'clock. It's the time for his stroll!—he's gone out!

ROYER-COLLARD

(pursuing the conversation begun)

No, Mr. Director, no! This man is not insane! Take your responsibilities! As, for me, head doctor, I've taken mine, by demanding, on the second of August, last, to Milord the General in Charge of The Ministry of Police that he find another place of confinement for Mr. de Sade, than the Charenton Hospital! I explained to His Excellency why—

DIRECTOR

Why, I know, Mr. Royer-Collard, I know—

ROYER-COLLARD

(with authority)

Well! I repeat to you! Mr. de Sade is not insane! His only delirium is that of vice—and it is not in a house dedicated to the medical treatment of insanity that that type of delirium can be restrained—

(in the corridors the howlings of the mad which had abated resume. A pause)

DIRECTOR

Still, that woman who was arrested at the same time, who was brought directly here? Number 8?

ROYER-COLLARD

La Fanchon? Why she is mad—indubitably! The padded cell for her!

DIRECTOR

As for him. transferred first to the Prison of Saint Pélagie, he was recognized as mad.

ROYER-COLLARD

What a mistake!

DIRECTOR

And interned at Bicetre.

ROYER-COLLARD

(concluding)

—Who knew how to rid themselves of him by sending him to us. The regime was stricter and Mr. de Sade has powerful protection!—feminine protection—notably Madame Delphine de Tarde, who employs herself on his behalf in high places.

DIRECTOR

(with an impotent gesture)

Possibly!— And what do you intend to do!

ROYER-COLLARD

(forceful)

Sequester him! That man is in a perpetual state of libertine dementia! It's necessary that a patient who has reached his state be isolated, to shelter others from corruption and first of all himself, from objects that could exalt his vice—

DIRECTOR

(with a smile)

Mr. Doctor in Chief, you are exaggerating!

ROYER-COLLARD

(raising his voice)

The house of Charenton, in the case in question doesn't fill either condition. Mr. de Sade has too great a liberty! I have written to the minister: the archives will prove it! (sitting down) Mr. de Sade has the right to communicate with patients, to receive them in his room, he preaches his horrible doctrines to some—(looking at the books on the table) He loans books to others—

DIRECTOR

(cautiously)

But—

ROYER-COLLARD

(reading the titles of the books)

And what books—*Justine*! *The Philosophy in the Boudoir*! A complete bouquet of poison! You've tolerated his creating a theatre in this house, under the pretext of playing comedies for the insane!

DIRECTOR

To distract them—

ROYER-COLLARD

It's a shame! And Mr. de Sade is the director of the theatre—he's the one who distributes the roles, presides over the rehearsals—

DIRECTOR

He's performed the task marvelously!

ROYER-COLLARD

(ironically)

Yes! At a party for the director, or the minister, or the archbishop, he has carefully composed a play in their honor—or some couplets praising them! (getting indignant) My reports, my demands to superior authority have remained vain! Mr. de Sade, strengthened by your singular benevolence, and strengthened by secret support has become the master, the true master here!

DIRECTOR

I protest, doctor, I protest! And nothing until now, nothing—

ROYER-COLLARD

Yes!—until the day when the scandal explodes. Then it will be too late to prevent the crime—but here he is.

(De Sade appears in the corridor)

DIRECTOR

It's he you wish to see, I am leaving you.

(He leaves by the left. De Sade holds an open book in his hand, and reads as he walks. He's seen Royer-Collard, and returns to his book, affecting not to see him. He slowly comes forward on stage. De Sade sits at a table and reads as if the doctor wasn't there. Royer-Collard silently looks at him. A pause, then de Sade, annoyed by this staring, closes his book angrily and brutally breaks the ice.)

DE SADE

(ironically and cold)

You are coming to get news of me, doctor? My health is marvelous! And you? What are they saying in Paris? His Majesty is still wining battles? Here, everything's going fine! (pause) Ah! I advise you less harshness for Number 15—you know perfectly—Number 15, the old Jacobin? It's when he had his reason—all his reason and when he had heads cut off every morning, they forgot to pass him straightjacket! And now—Oh! Oh! And Number 8 That Fanchon? I knew her! The padded cell? Why? Dangerous? for whom? for you? She foams and grinds her teeth at the sight of you. She recoils and trembles when I pass. But you hear nothing about the mad! (he bursts into laughter) The straightjacket! The padded cell!

(He raises his arms to heaven, laughing. He sits on the bed to the right. A silence. Royer-Collard observes him.)

ROYER-COLLARD

Watch out, you, don't end up in the padded cell!

DE SADE

I won't give you that joy! I am not mad!

ROYER-COLLARD

(acquiescing)

Merely criminal!

(De Sade Bursts into laughter)

DE SADE

Criminal? (a pause with scathing irony, little by little exalting) Ah, how young you are, sir! Look at my grey hair! Do you actually know that I lived under three regimes? I was a lieutenant, sir, during the Seven Years War—I emerged from college and I saw fields of battle—dead, blood! Criminal? (he rises) From 1789 to 1795 where were you, sir? In Paris? Did you see the powdered heads balancing atop pikes? and the red streams gushing? Did you see the Swiss, the nobles, pulled from the prisons, hacked up, mutilated, disemboweled?

(At this moment, a deafening sound of the madmen in the corridor, which reaches a crescendo and then subsides)

Did you see the mass murders? Did you see Fouquier, Couthon, Carrier, the shootings, the drownings—did you see them? Did you see 1500 heads roll in two weeks? Me, Criminal? What about the rest of them, sir? Criminal? Ask His Majesty Bonaparte how many soldiers he kills every day in the four corners of Europe? Criminal? Why, all history is a crime! See, piracy, wars, revolutions! History, glory? There you have it! Criminal? In that case, by God, I want my statue in the square.!

ROYER-COLLARD

Or in the courtyard of a prison? Would you like it?

DE SADE

(sitting down with a smile)

Having seen, sir, all that, are you sure that killing is a crime? And that from the point of view of the infinite, we are worth any more, you, I—than this earth worm, that we, mankind are worth more than animals? We put them to death without pity! Or the plant we tear out? Are you sure? What pride! As for me, no! To kill, why that's the law of nature—what does murder, hate teach—and even the plague gratifies us! We live by the death of others, animals or plants. Nothing dies—and everything transforms itself—

VOICE OF THE JACOBIN

To Death! To Death! Kill him! Kill him! Kill! Kill!

DE SADE

(rising and sneering)

Hear him! The Jacobin!

OTHER MADMEN

Ah! Ah! Enough! To Death! Kill him! Enough!

DE SADE

(won over, in his turn by the furious agitation)

Ah! Ah! Enough! Ah!

(goes toward the back and howls with the rest)

ROYER-COLLARD

(stupefied, he watches him and goes quickly to him)

You are not mad—and yet—

DE SADE

(getting control of himself, gnawing his lips and still trembling from his past crisis)

Yet?

ROYER-COLLARD

(a silence) (examining him)

Nothing! Nothing! I am awaiting with curiosity, the day of your death—

DE SADE

Of my death?

ROYER-COLLARD

The day when—we will be able to study—(he places his finger on de Sade's face) This monstrous brain!

DE SADE

(with a sort of horror)

Ah! indeed!— I don't want it!—d'you hear? I don't want it! My brain! What, prey, huh, for the disciples of Gall? You won't find anything, just a bit of love, a bit of hate!—of virtue, who knows? Of vice! A man's skull (with horror) I don't want it! I don't want it!

ROYER-COLLARD

(cutting him off)

You are afraid?

DE SADE

(continuing)

Society muzzled me during my life! It has no rights over my cadaver!

ROYER-COLLARD

(ironically)

In that case you are not afraid of hell?

DE SADE

(getting exalted)

Hell? Why, I'm in it, in hell, by your order—with madmen—monsters, demons! (head in his hands) Poisons of the soul! Hell? That's you, doctor, jailors, that's you! (howling, almost with fury) It's you! It's you! (to his bellowing, other madmen offstage respond. Again Royer-Collard starts to call. De Sade controls himself, and in a raucous voice) No! No! Unnecessary to call! Death? Freedom? I demand it! I'm waiting for it! I don't want them to steal it from me! As for you, sir, you are not atheistic? You believe in God, right? And the soul? Then. You respect the will of the dead? Well, here's my will!

(He opens a drawer in the table, takes a piece of paper and unfolds it.)

Listen up, Mr. Royer-Collard! (reading in a bitter voice): "I forbid that my body be opened under any pretext whatever! I demand that it be kept forty-eight hours in the cell where I shall die, placed in a wooden bier which will be nailed up only after the prescribed forty-eight hours—"

ROYER-COLLARD

(ironically)

Still afraid? Ah, indeed!

DE SADE

(continuing)

"...During this interval, a telegram will be sent to Sieur Normand, woodseller, boulevard of Equality, number 101, at Versailles, begging him to come with a tumbril to fetch my body, which he will transport to the forest on my land at Malmaison, near Épernon, where I intend that it be interred without any special ceremony, in the first clump of woods that he finds to the right of the aforesaid forest."

(he stops)

ROYER-COLLARD

That's all?

DE SADE

My pen stopped there.

(he places the will on the table. At this moment there

is uproar of voices in the corridor. The Guard appears at the back.)

THE WARDER

They are coming for their lesson! (to the mad, in the corridor) Come on—come closer! And be calm!

(The lunatics enter two by two, First, the priest, who is very old, dressed in a soutane that is in shreds, mumbling prayers, a rosary in his hand, then Madame de Rochebrune, old lady of lofty bearing; then the Jacobin, hideous, haggard, overexcited, La Dubois with a shrewish face; Marie with the eyes of a hysteric; Micoulet who strides with jerky motion; finally Justine with the face and laugh of a cretin. Each keeps his particular character aggravated by tics. The Warder makes them enter then moves away into the corridor)

THE JACOBIN

(singing between his teeth)

Ah! It's happenin'! It's happenin'! It's happenin'!

Aristocrats to the lamp posts! Ah! It's happenin'!.

LA DUBOIS

(at the same time)

For certain I will say it! Enough or I'll whack you!

Starver! Bold! The Knitters!

MICOULET

(military bearing, roguish)

One! Two! One! Two! Who is it sent me a draftee like this!

MARIE

(with eyes wandering)

Enough! Enough! You are making me ill! You are breaking my ears! I don't want to hear you! It's not you! It's not you!

DE SADE

Hush! (they shut up and become motionless) I am teaching them little couplets in honor of Monsignor the Archbishop whom we are receiving Sunday!

MADAME DE ROCHEBRUNE

(she takes a step out of the group and with intense emotion)

Gentlemen—I beg you! If a little humanity remains to you—If everything is not abolished! Pity! Mr. de Rochebrune is awaiting me! Spur on, coachman! It's you, Jacques? And first of all, doctor, it's not possible they can afflict me with this torture—these songs of hate! Who? The people? I am not mad! I have all my reason! Jacques! Jacques! Your mother is there—she's calling you! Help, my child! (she weeps)

PRIEST

(advancing towards her, with a distracted air, and pulling her away to the left, with his hands raised to heaven, as if leading her to the scaffold)

In saecula saeculorum.

DE SADE

(bowing ceremoniously before the priest)

I present you my duties, monsignor.

(turning toward the doctor while Justine laughs with an idiot's fitful laugh)

How to explain, doctor, the strange empire I have over them? Kindness? I obtain more from them through kindness than others—

(he turns towards the mad folks and brutally) by means of the straightjacket!

MARIE

(with a great shriek of terror)

Ah!

THE MAD FOLK

(they all scream and gnash their teeth and recoil in a great motion)

Ah! Ah! Ah! No! Ah! No! Ah! Ah! Ah!

(The priest with a leap jumps onto the bed naked arms extended in terror)

DE SADE

(to the doctor, pointing to the mad)

The flotsam, doctor! The lamentable flotsam of torture! They endured, without dying of it, the horror of bloody times, and trembling now, at the mere name of the straightjacket!

(to the mad who continue to tremble, some clinging to the bars, others crouching on the ground near the bed, all breathless, terrorized)

Come, come, don't be afraid! You! The Jacobin! And, you, Marie—Justine! And you, priest! The martyr of your faith! Madame Rochebrune, calm down a little. A knitter, indeed? a skinny-minnie.

(to Micoulet who's hiding) Beat it, Micoulet! Let's go!

(the lunatics have one by one resumed their places)

(De Sade says to the doctor) I have succeeded miraculously! They are singing in tune! (he takes a stick from the table and beats a tune) With your permission! (he attacks) One! Two!

THE MAD FOLK

(singing in psalmic melody)

Like the son of the Eternal

With uncommon compassion,

In the appearance of a mortal

Coming to console our misfortune.

THE JACOBIN

(singing)

Ah! It's happenin', it's happenin',

Hang the aristocrats from the lamp posts.

ROYER-COLLARD

(shrugs his shoulders murmuring)

What a pity!

(And at the beginning of the singing leaves by door at the left. But as soon as Royer-Collard has left, de Sade stops beating the measure. His faces changes expression and becomes terrible, and suddenly, eyes injected with blood, interrupts them)

DE SADE

On your knees! On your knees, swine! Vile humanity! On your knees!

(he hurls himself on Marie and armed with his stick showers blows on her)

MARIE

Ah! Ah!

(All the madmen, terrorized, fall to their knees, in frightened postures)

DE SADE

(extending his fist toward them)

Ah! Executioners! (turning toward the door through which Royer-Collard left) Executioners!

(he waits a second with his head in his hand, then addressing the mad with unspeakable disgust)

Go! Stand up!—you are free!

JACOBIN

(rising, shining)

Liberty! Equality! Or death! (with gestures from a courtroom) Death! Death!

(one by one the mad folk have risen, haggard, and walk about at random like drunks; De Sade looks at them, sneering)

PRIEST

(who was lying flat on his belly on the bed, rises)

I*n te, Domine speravi! non confundar in aeternum—in justitia tua libera me!*

LA DUBOIS

Dig a ditch! And let me be buried alive in it!

MARIE

(hands extended toward De Sade and going to him, as in a dream)

It's you! It's you! Beloved!

(But she bumps into Dubois, who in a mad fury is going to take her by the throat.)

LA DUBOIS

Get away! Get away! Or I'll strangle you!

WARDER

(at this moment the Warder appears behind the grill and opens it)

Well, what's this? You are not singing?

DE SADE

(haughtily to the warder)

We need a voice for the ensemble! You gave me seven, I need eight. And a woman!

WARDER

Who?

DE SADE

Well! Eight! Eight—at random! (an idea swiftly crosses his mind) Number 8.

WARDER

La Fanchon! But—

DE SADE

But what?

WARDER

You have the director's authorization?

DE SADE

Yes! And for the concert, I am the director— (imperious) Number 8! (as the warder leaves by the back shrugging his shoulders) I am the master!

(to the mad, cane raised, in a threat)

You hear! The rest of you! The master!

(La Dubois with a laugh of rage comes and goes while Marie, Justine, Mme de Rochebrune, hover around de Sade, hands extended toward him in supplication)

LA DUBOIS

(with an atrocious laugh)

Eight! Eight! The citizeness in a cage! Ah! Ah! Is she cured, yes or no? Ah! I want to see her? She'll sing! By Jove! And she'll dance Tra la la. Ha ha ha!

JACOBIN

(with demented grandiloquence)

Eight! Eight, number eight!

(all the mad surround de Sade, supported by the table. They fight for his glance, his smile)

THE PRIEST

(going towards them with visionary gestures)

In those days, Jesus said to his disciples—

(he goes to the table, takes a book, and holds it as he would hold his parish bible. All the mad are grouped at the left, when the Warder reappears pushing La Fanchon on stage.)

WARDER

Here's number 8!

(The Warder has disappeared in the corridor. La Fanchon remains motionless, eyes fixed without seeing. She is dressed in rags. De Sade has shut the bars. He approaches her slowly and seizes her by the arm)

LA FANCHON

(with a little scream)

Ah!

DE SADE

Do you recognize me?

LA FANCHON

(distracted)

Yes—yes— He's not returned. Here I am all alone—all alone? (she points with her fingers to the mad) Oh! Why what's that—what's that? (she gets frightened) The Police! (she smiles) Ah, yes! Yes, police!

DE SADE

You don't recognize me?

LA FANCHON

Oh! yes—yes—! (she laughs)

MADAME DE ROCHEBRUNE

(exasperated)

Why, can't you see she is mad! She is mad! Enough!

(La Fanchon is still laughing)

THE JACOBIN

Ah! Good for nothing slut! Are you going to stop laughing! Enough! (he laughs in his turn, gnashing his teeth)

LA DUBOIS

Whip her ass! Bugger of a mad woman! Ah!

(She laughs. They all laugh nervously)

DE SADE

(making them shut up)

Hush! (he takes La Fanchon by the wrists) Fanchon! Look at me! Fanchon! (La Fanchon at the call of her name, raises her head) You were lying naked, on the white tablecloth (he raises his hand) The knife! (he touches La Fanchon on the shoulder, at the place of the wound) And there! (La Fanchon starts in shock) Ah! Ah! The blood was pouring out, all fresh from your shoulder! Dubourg! The torches! Dubourg! The torches!

LA FANCHON

(reliving the horror of the scene)

Ah! Ah! Ah! (she recoils, shocked to the front of the stage) Pity! Ah! Ah! Ah!

(All the lunatics following de Sade have come forward a little. They are behind him, restrained by him, like a growling pack, mouths open, fists closed.)

DE SADE

Tally-ho! Pack! Seize her! Seize her!

MADAME DE ROCHEBRUNE

(together with the lunatics)

Whip her! Whip her! Whip her! Driver!

LUNATICS

(leaning over La Fanchon)

Kill! Kill! Ah! Ah! Ah!

LA FANCHON

(is brought to ground howling furiously)

Ah! Ah! Ah!— Ah! Savage beasts—caught in a trap! (as to an invisible interlocutor) A beast? Who? Who? Me? Ah, it's not true!

DE SADE

(leaning over her)

Yes!

THE LUNATICS

(ditto)

Yes! Yes!

LA FANCHON

It's not true! Ah! I swear—sir, Ladies! Ah! They are taking me for a wild beast—a ferocious beast! (with rales of sorrow) Ah! evildoers! Ah! They are burning me! Ah! I'm ill. They are killing me. Oh! Oh! Stop! Stop! Why, I cannot be a wild beast, sir! (with bursts of tears) My name's Fanchon—yes, Fanchon—I live in the rue—

(The lunatics and de Sade punctuate each of her words with a sneer)

DE SADE

It's not true!

THE LUNATICS

(fists waved toward her, howling and laughing)

Not true! No! No! Not true!

(From the pushing and threats of the unchained pack, La Fanchon has risen, crossed the stage, pursued by de Sade and the lunatics. She's fought her way to the door. De Sade with his arms extended holds back the lunatics. The Priest, follows the group, furious, with his hands extended toward heaven)

LA FANCHON

Ah! The horror! The horror! Ah! They're tearing my soul from me—my skin! They're changing me into—into (she becomes speechless) I don't want it! I don't want it! (she pants, like an animal, rises, then falls back on her hands) Ah! Ah! Wild beast—I'm the—the female—wild beast! (she pants) Ah! Ah!

DE SADE

Look! Look! (La Fanchon crawls on all fours) She's crawling on all fours! (calling her) Here! (the lunatics sneer) Here! (she doesn't obey. De Sade yells threateningly) Dubourg!

(Fanchon on all fours drags herself to him, right up to his hand which she embraces. At the sight of this, the lunatics, now jealous, stamp their feet, howling.)

LUNATICS

Ah! Dirty trick! Ah! Dung! Bitch! Kill! Kill her! Let me! Let me!

THE JACOBIN

(hands near Fanchon's throat)

I'll kill her. I will! Here! I've got her.

DE SADE

(terrible, making them recoil, threatening them with his cane)

You are forbidden to touch her. (pointing to Fanchon) This animal belongs to me!

(Under the threat, the pack yells, recoils. Marie with a shocking howl, has opened the barred door. Marie, Justine, and Micoulet, and La Dubois are already in the corridor when the small door to the right opens and the Warder appears.)

WARDER

(in the doorway, calling brutally)

De Sade! A visitor for you!

(he steps back to let Delphine pass and disappears shutting the door. Delphine enters rapidly, subject to great agitation. She stops at the sight of the lunatics.)

DE SADE

Delphine! What a surprise!

(he goes to kiss her hand. Delphine stops him, in a voice trembling with rage)

DELPHINE

I need to talk to you! (with a sort of horror, pointing to the lunatics) Send them away!

DE SADE

They are inoffensive!

(With a gesture he makes the Jacobin, The Priest, and Madame Rochebrune who were still on stage leave. He shuts the barred door. But the lunatics do not go away at all. They remain by the gate. They watch through the bars, their faces shriveled, hideous. They are listening. They watch, curious, attentive. The priest is motionless, hands raised to heaven in a mystic ecstasy. Delphine comes forward, suddenly she notices, cowering near the table, La Fanchon, as the lunatics exit, recoils, and crouches there like a cornered animal.)

DELPHINE

And this one? (looking at her more attentively) Ah! Why—I'm not mistaken, it's—?

DE SADE

It's she!

DELPHINE

What a shock! (going to her with a gesture of pity)!

The poor child!

LA FANCHON

(getting up with a leap and a scream, backing away right up to the wall) Who is there?

DELPHINE

(with fright) Ah! God!

DE SADE

Well, yes! She is mad! (sneering) But the whole world is—everywhere, is mad—the whole world—!

DELPHINE

(looking at Fanchon)

Why look—see how she's staring at me—

LA FANCHON

(She runs around the cell, crouching against the walls, eyes fixed on Delphine) Get back!

DELPHINE

Her whole body is trembling with fury! Her hands look like claws!

(La Fanchon has reached the cell door behind whose bars the lunatics are crouching. Sneeringly, they pass their hands through the bars trying to grasp her. She escapes them and goes to the bed where she crouches down.)

DE SADE

I've changed her into one of the Furies! She thinks, in her dementia, she's become a ferocious animal! She has become a ferocious animal. But since I am here, don't be afraid!— What have you to say to me that's so serious, Delphine?

DELPHINE

(in a dull voice, throat dry)

Ah! I came here with the intention of ending it—yes. The intention to know! With rage, and disgust, too! And now—after I've got here—

THE LUNATICS

(behind the bars)

Ah! Ah! Open-up! Ah! Ah!

LA FANCHON

(as the lunatics sneer, in a low voice like a bitch howling over the dead)

Ah! Ah! Ah!

DELPHINE

(continuing)

...In the midst of these creatures—and with you! a horror is seizing me. This is Hell! And I'm suffocating—in these shadows! I no longer have the words I need—I am stupefied—annihilated. (she falls onto a stool)

LUNATICS

(calling)

Psst! Hey! Hey! Hey, there!

THE JACOBIN

KILL! To Death! Kill!

LA FANCHON

(as the lunatics speaks, she hallucinates, pointing to her hands, then the ground)

Blood! Blood! There! There!

DE SADE

(calm, responding to Delphine)

You came to her in a rage, you say? Speak! Explain yourself!

DELPHINE

(she rises and holds out to him the libel that she grasps in her hand)

Do you know this filthy libel—which is running all over Paris? It accuses Fouché of complaisance regarding you—it accuses him of servilely obeying your friends, La Saint Ange and—And me—me! Read—what your enemies are saying about me!

DE SADE

Are they insulting you?

DELPHINE

Worse than that! There! There! There! (hiding her face in horror) Beneath the title: Tearing away the veil!

DE SADE

(reading): "And this Delphine de Tarde—that Fouché receives and is eager to serve—who is she? a creature that the author of Justine (De Sade bows ironically) raised in his school—the school of vice—that he defiled, corrupted to please himself—that he made participate in his orgies—who became, for absolute certain, his mistress. (up to this point he has read, punctuating each phrase with a smile. But now he stops and after having read silently, or in a murmur reads aloud, as if to himself) And she's his daughter—the natural daughter of the Marquis de Sade! (he rips up the libel, brutally as he finishes the last phrase)

DELPHINE

(extending towards him)

Scream that it's false! This infamy! Scream that it's false!

DE SADE

(passing to the left, sneering)

Oh! Oh! The Oedipus of Mr. Voltaire!

DELPHINE

Answer!

DE SADE

(turning towards her—and violently)

Your mother was La Gouran!

DELPHINE

(in a scream of anguish)

And my father?

DE SADE

(striding to her)

What do you mean by father? The carefree brute who procreated or—actually—

DELPHINE

Wretch!

DE SADE

Or rather the educator who loves you!

DELPHINE

(threatening him, crazed with anger, pain, and rage)

I hate you! Don't you see the abyss into which we are falling—the abyss!

DE SADE

(pushing her away violently)

Ah, indeed! Are you going mad, too?

(Behind the bars, the lunatics are agitated, excited by the uproar of the dispute. Delphine and De Sade don't see La Fanchon approach. At Delphine's first screams, La Fanchon stands up, growing in a raucous scream "Enough! Enough! I don't want it! Enough!" she advances, crawling on her hands and knees)

DELPHINE

(responding to de Sade)

Deliver me from this horror! Take my life! Kill me! (she never finishes; La Fanchon hurls herself on her, takes her by the throat. Delphine struggles, weakens and falls to her knees under the furious assault of the mad woman. The lunatics behind the gate extend their hands, screaming "Kill! Kill! To death!"

DE SADE

(wanting to release Delphine, to la Fanchon)

Get away, or I'll beat you, Fury!

(But suddenly his face changes Nailed to the spot, abruptly dominated by the cruel instinct of madness, he looks with a monstrous joy as La Fanchon strangles Delphine. He laughs, laughs frightfully. It only lasts a minute. He comes to himself! Too late! Delphine does not budge and La Fanchon furiously attacks a cadaver)

Criminal that I am! Criminal!

(He's overwhelmed, and collapses on the stool. And on

the table in front of him he sees the will—and begins to read): "In the first copse to the right!"

THE PRIEST

(coming forward to the first ranks behind the bars, and with his hands raised, pulling at the bars he intones the prayer for the dead): *De profundis clamavi ad te! Domine!*

(La Fanchon has backed away, panting to the wall of the cell, where eyes enlarged by horror, she remains motionless. De Sade has taken the pen and with an accent of despair finishes the will he began.)

DE SADE

(writing)

"So that the copse having grown—the traces of my tomb will vanish beneath the surface of the earth."

(a distant clock can be heard ringing grave and dull.)

THE PRIEST

(intoning)

Requiem aeternum donna eis, Domine!

DE SADE

(Continuing as the clock rings):

"...As I flatter myself that my memory will be effaced from the mind of men."

LUNATICS

(behind the bars)

Ah! Ah! Open! Me! Me! Ah! Ah!

(while the lunatics, hideous and grimacing, stamp and are agitated, La Fanchon in a raucous voice hovers over the dead. And behind the bars, the vision of hell will last until the falling of the curtain, as the clock continues to ring, and de Sade finishes writing.)

DE SADE

"...Done at Charenton-Saint Maurice—in a state of reason—and health." (signing) De Sade

(slowly the curtain falls. The Priest intones)

THE PRIEST

Et lux perpetua luceat eis!

CURTAIN

ABOUT THE AUTHOR

Frank J. Morlock has written and translated many plays since retiring from the legal profession in 1992. His translations have also appeared on Project Gutenberg, the Alexandre Dumas Père web page, Literature in the Age of Napoléon, Infinite Artistries. com, and Munsey's (formerly Blackmask). In 2006 he received an award from the North American Jules Verne Society for his translations of Verne's plays. He lives and works in México.

www.ingramcontent.com/pod-product-compliance
Lightning Source LLC
LaVergne TN
LVHW011214080426
835508LV00007B/779

* 9 7 8 1 4 3 4 4 3 5 5 5 2 *